"Witty writing, trustworthy research, forceful opinions, and perfect illustrations. You won't find a better overview of curry and curry politics than this."
—Rachel Laudan, author of *Cuisine and Empire: Cooking in World History*

"*The Philosophy of Curry* is Sejal Sukhadwala's marvellous, rollicking history of how one simply-named spiced dish finds its origin in extraordinary Indian cooking, while also representing the best and worst of British society's view of India, and its diaspora, through a complex cuisine and heritage."
—Dan Lepard, chef and author of *The Handmade Loaf*

"A fascinating, deftly-told journey through the rich and complex history of the curry."
—Jenny Linford, author of *The Missing Ingredient: The Curious Role of Time in Food and Flavour*

"In this gorgeously illustrated book, Sukhadwala dives head-long into the discussion of whether curry should be cancelled due to its association with colonialism and use as a limiting stereotype for the vast range of South Asian dishes. She delivers her response with terrific writing and panache."
—Krishnendu Ray, Chair of the Department of Nutrition and Food Studies, New York University

T0021006

THE PHILOSOPHY OF
CURRY

THE PHILOSOPHY OF
CURRY

SEJAL SUKHADWALA

First published 2022 by
The British Library
96 Euston Road
London NW1 2DB

ISBN 978 0 7123 5450 9
eISBN 978 0 7123 6774 5
Cataloguing in Publication Data
A catalogue record for this book is available
from the British Library

Designed and typeset by Sandra Friesen
Printed in the Czech Republic by Finidr

CONTENTS

INTRODUCTION

Curry is strongly associated with Indian food – so much so that as an Indian I can barely talk to a stranger without being asked about curry ingredients and recipes. However, Indian curries don't even appear to be that popular any more. In a 2021 poll curry doesn't feature in the nation's top fifty-seven dishes, although in another questionnaire from the same year, Indian was the second most-loved takeaway after Chinese, above fish and chips. In a worldwide survey of twenty-four countries in 2019, Indian was only the fourth cuisine of choice in Britain after British, Italian and Chinese. And chicken tikka masala is no longer Britain's top curry – a 2016 vote put chicken korma at number one.[1]

Moreover, in a CNN Travel survey of the World's Fifty Best Foods updated in 2021,[2] there are three curries to be found, but none are Indian: South Africa's bunny chow, Indonesian rendang and Thai massaman, which came in at number one. I know these ballots can be arbitrary and only a tiny population of the world votes in them, but they can also be a useful barometer of changing tastes. The Indian dishes on the CNN list are in fact masala dosa and garlic butter crab, which would surely please the 'curry deniers' no end.

Curry deniers are Indians, often from the diaspora, who hate the term 'curry'. During the writing of this book a controversy erupted when an American-Indian 'influencer' urged people to 'cancel the word because of its association with colonialism'.[3] It was a clumsily worded statement, but it reflects a growing resentment of the use of the word. 'But there's no such thing as curry!' was a common response when some Indian acquaintances heard I was writing this book. One even helpfully suggested I drop the word 'curry' from the title and write a book on philosophy instead.

Perhaps it was Madhur Jaffrey who fired the first shot by writing in 1973's *An Invitation to Indian Cooking*:

> To me the word 'curry' is as degrading to India's great cuisine as the term 'chop suey' was to China's … 'Curry' is just a vague, inaccurate word which the world has picked up from the British, who, in turn, got it mistakenly from us… If 'curry' is an oversimplified name for an ancient cuisine, then 'curry powder' attempts to oversimplify (and destroy) the cuisine itself.[4]

Jaffrey later changed her mind because she went on to write the *Ultimate Curry Bible*, and other cookbooks with the word 'curry' in their title.

The argument is that the word dumbs down a hugely complex and varied cuisine into one catch-all term that doesn't reflect regional diversity. There's so much more to Indian food than curries: dumplings, pancakes, stir-fries, noodles, fritters, savoury porridges and an enormous variety of snacks and street foods. Additionally curry is only one of many genres of dishes in a *thali*, comprising flatbreads, rice, dal or another legume, meat or another protein, vegetables, pickles and relishes.

In ancient India rice was the main dish: it was piled up high on a plate, and the savoury accompaniments – no distinction was made between sauced dishes and pickles – were only eaten in tiny quantities like relishes. Then Europeans came along, turning the rice:relish ratio the other way around and, it seems, randomly singling out one category of dishes for special attention. They could have chosen dal, a staple in every Indian household, or rice – which was cooked in increasingly clever, complex and competitive ways in Mughlai kitchens – but instead they shone a light on curry. One reason they did so is because they were used to eating meat cooked in a different way – roasted, boiled or baked – and they found the method of cooking small pieces of meat on a stove top fascinating.

Many Indians are also keen to distance themselves from what they regard as 'downmarket Bangladeshi curry houses', which they associate with greasy curries and use of food colouring, with some expressing anger about restaurants misrepresenting 'real Indian home cooking'.

But it is curry's association with colonialism that is the biggest problem. One curry denier asked me recently: 'Why should I call a dish curry just because a British coloniser called Mr Curry loved Indian food so much that someone decided to name it after him?' Although curry does have an association with colonialism, this speculation is incorrect.

For others it brings back painful memories of being told by other schoolchildren in the playground that they smell of curry – the kind of racism that persists even today for adults living in apartment blocks in some European cities, who've been told not to cook curry in case the smell offends their neighbours.

But here's the thing. For every Indian who says they didn't grow up using the word curry or buying curry powder there are many others who did. Each Indian person's experience is limited to that within their own family, so generalisations about the widely varying food habits of other communities are pointless.

In India curries are often called 'gravy' or 'masala', and may be referred to as 'restaurant-style' or 'hotel-style'. The word has South Indian origins, as we'll see in the next chapter, but the most common type of restaurant food in India is Punjabi or Mughlai (South Indian restaurants have a different history based on temple food and the mass feeding of pilgrims).

So in India curry frequently refers to North Indian dishes, often cooked in a tomato and onion-based gravy. Regional curries are known by specific names like sabzi, shaak, salna, salan, palya, poriyal, fry, jhol, rassa, kuzhambu, saagu, erissery, gassi, pulusu and so on. These are all varieties of curries named after ingredient, consistency, texture or technique.

BAWARCHI. (COOK.)

WHAT IS CURRY?

AT ITS MOST basic a curry is a spiced stew with a gravy cooked in a pot. This isn't entirely accurate because a curry may be dry – though as it's then called a 'dry curry', it shows that wet curries are the norm. In modern times, curries can also be baked in a casserole or as a traybake.

Moreover spicy stews are not always curry – North African tajines and Ethiopian and Eritrean wats spring to mind. Even within Indian cuisine, not all dishes with a spiced gravy are curries. I don't consider lentil-based dals and sambars to be curries – though some Indians do call them 'lentil curries'.

The best I can come up with is this: curry is a spiced dish of Indian origin or influence, in which vegetables, or meat or other protein, are normally cooked in a pot, usually with a gravy made from tomatoes, onions, coconut, yoghurt, gram flour, nuts, cream, water or stock. I know this definition isn't entirely adequate, but I have tried to cover all bases.

The word is associated with British colonialism, but in fact it dates back even further to the Portuguese in Goa in the sixteenth century. The Portuguese physician Garcia de Orta (1501–1568) observed Indians' eating habits in *Conversations On the Simples, Drugs and Medicinal Substances of India* (1563), writing that 'they made dishes of fowl and flesh, which they call caril'.

Various food historians have claimed over the centuries that curry comes from the Tamil word *kari*, which means either black pepper, spices generally, a spiced accompaniment to rice, a sauce, sautéed meat and vegetable dishes, or 'to eat by biting', depending on who you ask. They have also claimed that the word has roots not only in Tamil, but also in the Kannada and Malayalam languages.

The sixteenth-century Portuguese historians and travellers then adapted *kari* into *caril* – one theory being that *caril* is the Kannada word for Tamil *kari*; another that the Portuguese *caril* was singular, and its plural *carie* or *curree* became the English word 'curry'. The British applied 'curry' as a generic term for spiced South Indian accompaniments made from thin broth, chunky gravy or no gravy, all of which had specific names and were traditionally served in courses one after another.

Henry Yule and A. C. Burnell, authors of Anglo-Indian dictionary *Hobson-Jobson* (1886), even mischievously suggested that when the Europeans used the word curry, they weren't necessarily referring to an Indian dish, but the spiced dishes of medieval Europe and Asia, which were coloured like a curry with saffron and sandalwood. This wholly speculative 'curries were actually European' idea could lead to a wild new narrative.

To try to reconcile these contradictory theories I consulted a translation website, which gave me the word 'charcoal' for *kari*. I then asked Tamil-speaking South Indian food historian Ammini Ramachandran for clarification, who confirmed that yes, *kari* does mean charcoal – but it's a word with multiple meanings and pronounced in two different ways in Tamil and Malayalam, with a different emphasis on the letter 'r'.

In both languages it's a generic term for a wide variety of vegetable and meat dishes cooked in a spicy liquid – including pickles. For example, *ellukari* is a dish of vegetables cooked in a sesame gravy, *pulinkari* are vegetables in a tamarind gravy, *maangakari* is mango pickle and *naarangakari* is lemon pickle. Ramachandran further explained that *kari* also refers to the colour black. Because of this, gravies in which black pepper was the main spice are prefaced with the word *kari* – for instance *kari moloshyam*, a vegetable curry in black pepper and coconut gravy.

So the Portuguese and then the British may have turned *kari* or *caril* into curry, but they didn't just pluck it out of thin air – the word still has Indian roots. To add to the intrigue there are several curry-like words in other Indian languages that all mean curry: Gujarati Bohra Muslim *kaari*, Andhra *koora*, the East Indian Christian community's *khudi*, Konkani *upkari* and North Indian *tarkari*, to name a few.

Some Indians also call *kadhi* – a gram flour-based broth with regional variations that may include yoghurt, vegetables or pakoras – a curry, but for me it's a separate category of dishes. All of this just goes to show that we can debate what a curry is and isn't forever – as has been done for centuries.

EARLIEST INDIAN CURRIES

CURRIES ARE MENTIONED often in ancient Indian literature or writings about India. There are references to white rice served with curried crabs and vegetables in prehistoric India.[5] There's also a detailed description of a picnic in the *Mahabharata* (written between 400 BC and the second century), which mentions curries among several other meat preparations: 'Clean cooks, under the supervision of diligent stewards, served large pieces of meat roasted on spits; meat cooked as curries and sauces made of tamarind and pomegranate …' During the Aryan era (1800–1500 BC), Hindu sects such as the Kanyakubjas in Uttar Pradesh served rice and vegetable curries at weddings.

An early reference to curry-like dishes comes from the Greek historian Megasthenes (350–290 BC), who wrote in his travelogue titled *Indica*: 'Among the Indians, at a banquet, a table is set before each individual … and on the table is placed a golden dish on which they throw, first of all, boiled rice … and then they add many sorts of meat dressed after the Indian fashion.' Another historic observation was in AD 477 in the *Mahavanso*, in which a Brahmin named Kassapo 'partook of rice dressed in butter, with its full accompaniment of curries'. The *Mahavanso*, also known as the *Mahavamsa* or *Mahawanso*, is a chronicle of the ancient kings of Ceylon, once a part of India.

In *Indian Food: A Historical Companion*, K. T. Achaya (1923–2002) describes one of the earliest recorded recipes for a curry in the second century AD:

> Blending of pulses along with vegetables and meat to give curries was practised; thus mung dhal, pieces of lotus stalk, and chironji seeds were seasoned with asafoetida and green ginger pieces, fried in oil, and boiled to a curry, to which might have been added fried brinjal pieces, mutton, jackal meat or even animal marrow, the dish being finished with black pepper and dry ginger: an elaborate concoction truly fit for a king.[6]

The earliest cooking methods in India included dehydrating, boiling, parboiling, braising, steaming, pan-frying, deep-frying, dry-roasting, grilling and baking. Slow-cooking over a low heat came later, around 1500 BC, and can be attributed to the use of cow dung as fuel, as it burned more evenly at a lower temperature.

India's hot climate meant freshly killed meat had to be cooked immediately, over a gentle heat for a long time to make it soft; it could not be hung up to tenderise as in

cooler climates otherwise it would spoil. Cooking pots with rounded bottoms (to give room for fat and spices to accumulate), oil production on a commercial scale and grinding stones all developed one after another, creating the implements and conditions for making a curry.

Travellers to India in the sixteenth and seventeenth centuries also described royal curries in lavish detail. The Portuguese writer Duarte Barbosa (1480–1521) wrote in his

1516 *Book of Duarte Barbosa* about the Rajah of Calicut's meal: 'Attendants ... brought in a large silver tray on which were placed empty silver saucers. On another low stool was placed a copper pot of cooked rice. A pile of rice was heaped on a plate, and curried meat, sauces and chutneys placed in the saucers.'

Another observation comes from the British cleric Reverend Samuel Purchas (1575–1626) in *Purchas, His Pilgrim* (1619): 'They feed not freely on full dishes of mutton and beef, as we, but much on rice boiled with pieces of flesh or dressed many other ways. They have not many roast or baked meats, but stew most of their flesh.'

In contrast to these extravagant curries, the cleric Reverend Edward Terry (1590–1660) noted in *A Voyage to East-India* (1655) that the poor didn't eat curry; instead they mostly lived on flatbreads, occasionally boiling rice with fresh ginger, black pepper and butter.

It's important to bear in mind that the word 'curry' in the above instances mostly comes from travellers and translators, and it's not always clear what the original word was. Except in one instance: 'curry' in the *Mahavanso* was translated in the nineteenth century by the book's editor George Turnour (1799–1843) from the Pali word *sūpa*, which means soup. So it's possible that in ancient India, curries were in fact soups, which only adds to the mystery of their origins.

INDIAN FOOD

FROM PREHISTORIC TIMES
TO THE COLONIAL ERA

IT'S WELL KNOWN that Indian cuisine is highly regional, but that's only half the story. It's not only that the food of each one of its current twenty-eight states and eight union territories is extremely diverse, but also that the food of one city can differ dramatically from that of its neighbouring city. The cooking of every religion, sect, caste, sub-caste, ethnic group and community group is different.

Additionally the ingredients and flavour combinations in old recipes came from Indian medicinal principles of Ayurveda, based on 'hot' and 'cold' properties of foods and the effect they have on the body – for instance adding asafoetida to bean dishes to prevent wind. This was further complicated by the theory of six *rasas* – six tastes comprising salty, sour, pungent, astringent, bitter and sweet. As if this weren't enough, there are lengthy doctrines about pure and impure foods, and rituals that dictate what is and isn't allowed. And this is before we even get to the intricacies of religious fasting. Things are changing, however, and fewer Indians today follow stringent culinary rules.

India was originally an assortment of individual sects and groups with a shared way of living, until semi-nomadic Indo-European tribes moved from the Caucasus region into North India in 2000 BC and introduced the early stages of Hinduism and the caste system. They cultivated wheat, millet and rice, and used ghee, milk and yoghurt in large quantities.

In prehistoric India rice and barley were cultivated, alongside a wide variety of beans and lentils. Indigenous fruit and vegetables included mangoes, jackfruit, bananas, a variety of lemons, coconuts, aubergines, pumpkins and gourds. The earliest spices were turmeric, fresh and dried ginger, coriander, holy basil and garlic. They're not all necessarily native to India, but they are often mentioned in the old texts and arrived in India early, if not found in their wild forms already. Others included green and black cardamom,

Pimienta negra.

Hoja

cumin, fenugreek, cloves, nutmeg, mace, cinnamon, cassia and *tej patta* (the leaves of the cassia tree). A variety of peppers grew in abundance, including black pepper, long pepper and the lesser-known *cubeb* or Java pepper.

The early Indians ate meat, including beef, and were the first to domesticate the jungle fowl; vegetarianism based on the principles of non-violence was introduced when

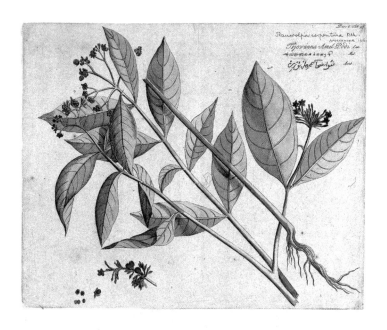

Buddhism and Jainism formed around 500 BC. These tribes grew into kingdoms and empires, and an extremely wealthy India was exporting spices as early as 300 BC to the Roman Empire, the Persian Gulf, Central Asia, China and Southeast Asia.

In the eighth century AD Arab traders set up colonies on the west coast. Meanwhile Central Asia's Islamic tribes began invading Northwest India, establishing power by the mid-thirteenth century. Turks, Afghans and Central Asian tribes ruled over most of India for a few hundred years. Mongol (from which the word Mughlai derives) Genghis Khan's descendent Babur invaded North India in 1526 – where Muslim sultans from Turkey, Persia and Afghanistan had already been ruling. This launched a Mughal dynasty that commanded large parts of North India until the eighteenth century and beyond.

It was during Babur's era, and particularly after his return from a fifteen-year exile in 1555 when he brought back cooks and influences from the highly sophisticated kitchens of Persia, that the cuisine we now call Mughlai was born. Persians introduced rosewater, saffron and many famous meat curries such as korma, kofta and dopiaza; Afghanistan and Central Asia brought asafoetida, almonds, pistachios, raisins, sultanas, dried figs and dried apricots. Jewish settlers introduced sugar and pomegranates.

Hindu food had been somewhat austere and pious until Islamic influence brought a more polished, decadent attitude towards the pleasures of eating. Hindus had an established caste system by now, and upper-caste Brahmins shunned meat, onions and garlic, which were believed to arouse passions. Muslims popularised not only these, but also ghee, dairy and a wider range of spices including saffron. Indian cooks imbuing the Mughal court's Persian dishes and the Central Asian tribes' recipes with their own local spices served to lay the first foundations of Mughlai cuisine.

However, it was during the time of the third emperor Akbar (1556–1605) that this new style of cooking really came into its own. Cooks from Islamic countries around

the world, as well as local chefs, competed or collaborated to create fantastical dishes full of wonder, splendour, humour, incredible aesthetics and the kind of eye-popping techniques that wouldn't look out of place in the kitchens of today's most cutting-edge chefs.

Some Mughlai curry ingredients and recipes were recorded in a hugely significant sixteenth-century tome, *Ain I Akbari* by the court writer Abu'l-Fazi ibn Mubarak, including yakhni, dopiaza, kalia and dum pukht. Persian

influences included cooking with *keema* or minced meat (a way of tenderising its flesh), using sugar as a spice in savoury dishes, applying an array of natural food colours, marinating meat in yoghurt, thickening curries with ground almonds and adding copious quantities of onions and garlic. Another Persian practice was cooking meat with fresh and dried fruit and spices – already prevalent in Arab-influenced medieval European cooking familiar to the British, who later went on to add apples and sultanas to their curries.

Meanwhile South Indian cuisine was being shaped by immigrants and traders. The famous Kerala stew is said to have been introduced in the first century AD by Syrian Christians, who learned how to make it from Irish monks and adapted it into a mild, coconut-based curry to eat with *appams* (fermented rice and coconut pancakes).

In Hyderabad the cuisine was influenced by Persian Shi'ites and Deccan Hindus, who cooked curries, pulaos and later Mughal-influenced biryanis and kababs using local ingredients such as fresh coconut, curry leaves and tamarind. Hindu temples were instrumental in developing South Indian vegetarian dishes and later, in the twentieth century, served as templates for inexpensive, meat-free Udupi restaurants.

Arab traders controlled the lucrative spice trade until the fifteenth century, while Europeans had been looking for a way to break their monopoly. After the Fall of Constantinople the Portuguese explorer Vasco de Gama (1469–1524) arrived at Calicut on the Malabar Coast in 1498, establishing India's first European colony in Goa, which lasted until 1961. The new colonisers married local women and initially adopted Indian food habits and ate their food, before converting a large number of Hindus to Christianity.

Portuguese foods based on wheat, pork, lamb, beef, olive oil and assorted grape products – wine, vinegar, juice and verjuice – combined with South Indian ingredients such as locally grown spices, coconut, rice and tamarind shaped Goan cuisine. The Portuguese also introduced new techniques such as marinating and cooking with vinegar, while Saraswat Brahmins developed Hindu vegetarian cuisine separately. Goa became an international hub for exchanging fruits, vegetables, nuts and other edible plants between India, Africa, Europe, America and Australasia, in what became known as the Columbian Exchange.

There's no record in any travellers' books, early Sanskrit cookbooks or the *Ain I Akbari* of chillies in India before the sixteenth century; peppers, mustard and ginger were used for achieving heat until that point. The Portuguese are believed to have introduced chillies via the Columbian Exchange. As they were initially called Pernambuco pepper, which suggests a Brazilian connection, the early imports may have come from Brazil via Lisbon. In Bombay they were known as *Gowai mirchi*, or Goan pepper, so Goa is likely to have been their entry point.

By as late as the seventeenth century chillies were mostly used only in South Indian cuisines. South Indians already used a lot of long pepper, so they embraced chillies enthusiastically as the pods looked and tasted similar, grew easily and didn't become mouldy. Over time chillies replaced long pepper in Indian cooking, though black pepper still has a distinctive role. They were taken to North India by the Marathas, a chilli-loving community from the Deccan in Central India, who played a crucial role in the fall of the

C
Le temperament.
On peult suffisamment cognoistre des facultez d'icelle, & au goust, auqu̅
delaisse adstriction manifeste, que cest'herbe est chaulde & seche.

Les vertus extraictes de Dioscoride.
La decoction d'icelle boullie en vin, beue, donne allegeance a ceulx qui̅
fieure, a la difficulté d'vrine & au sengloust. Elle rompt la pierre en la vescie, &
uocque a vriner.

De Paul Egineta.
La Saxifrage esmeut l'vrine, & brise la pierre.

Du Siliquastre.   Chap. CCLXXX
Les noms.

A Est'herbe a esté competemment n̅omee de Plyne au vingtiesme
chapitre dixseptiesme Siliquastr̅u: a raison des grandes & longue̅
ques quelle porte. Icelle aussi d'elle mesme, s'est n̅omee Piperitis,
ce que sa graine quand au goust ha la saueur & l'acrimonie du po̅
Elle est ce neantmoins differente de celle que le vulgaire appelle
ritis, c̅ome deuant aussi auons admonesté. Aucuns la noment Piper Hispanu̅
autres, Piper Indianum: d'autres Piper ex Calechuth. Il semble que Auicenne
pelle Zinziber caninum. En Françoys Poyure d'Espaigne, ou d'Inde.

Les especes.
Il y a vng grand & vng petit Siliquastre.
Le plus grand porte grandes siliques,
noiratres ou brunes. Le plus petit, au con-
traire, moindres & violettes. Nous auons c̅o
pris soubz vne peincture, l'vng & l'autre, &
auons donné charge de peindre deux siliques entrebaillees, & quelque peu ouuer-
tes: non pas que naturellement elles se rom
pent ainsi, mais affin qu'on voye quelle se-
B mence est dedans c̅otenue. Oultre ces deux
genres, il en y a encore deux autres desquelz
l'vng porte treslongues siliques & punicees.
L'autre, les ha plus larges & plus courtes.
Nous te baillons doncques a present quatre
especes differentes de Siliquastre, ainsi que
l'on peult veoir manifestement par les pein-
ctures. Pour mieulx les distinguer auons ap
pellé se premier, le plus grand. Le second, le
moindre. Le tiers, le long: & le quart, le large Siliquastre.

La forme.
C'est vne herbe ayant la tige rouge & lon
gue, fort noueuse. La feuille de Laurier. Les
fleurs blanches. La semence blanche, ou
plus tost rousse & tenule, contenue dedans
siliques. Le goust de Poyure tressacré & mor
dicant. La racine simple, blanchatre & fibreu
se. De ceste description il est asses manifeste,
que l'herbe icy peincte est le vray Siliquastre de Plyne, ou Piperitis. Car elle ha la tige

Poyure d'Inde grand & peti

Long Siliquastre.   Large Siliquastre.

& longue, comme Plyne ha cuilly de Caftor: fort noueufe, de laquelle iffent
illes femblables a celles de Laurier. La graine blanche, & moult tenule, le
de Poyure. Auec toutes ces marcques on peult adioufter les diuerfitez des
, c'eft a fçauoir de Siliquaftre & Piperitis, lefquelz quadrent tresbien & con-
ent a ceft herbe.

Le lieu.

fia par tout en Alemaigne il fe garde & vient dedans potz de terre. Il n'y ha
ng temps, qu'il eftoit incogneu.

Le temps.

eurift en aifté, & non guere apres que la fleur eft tombee furuiennent les fili-
au commancement de couleur d'herbe, & puis rouffes ou brunes, toutes plei
e femence.

Le temperament.

fchaulfe vaillamment & defeche, ce que monftre euidemment l'exceffiue a-
nie de la graine & amertume des feuilles, tellement que non trop follement
urs vfent de ladicte graine en lieu de Poyure. Car fans doubte nulle, il ha pa-
s vertus, lefquelles cy apres defcrirons, les transferans de Diofcoride.

Les vertus extraictes de Diofcoride.

emierement Piperitis ha vertu d'efchaulfer, d'efmouuoir l'vrine, d'ayder a
a cuyffon, d'attirer, de diffouldre, & d'effacer tout ce qui obfcurcift la veue. La
Piperitis beue & appliquee par dehors, profite aux rigueurs & friffons retour
par certains interualles. Elle ayde aux morfures des beftes venimeufes. Elle
ftir l'enfant hors du ventre. Icelle prife en forme de looth & breuage, donne
                                                                    allegean

Mughals and the Portuguese, but were later defeated by the British.

The East India Company, set up to trade with India, became more powerful and established trading posts on the east and west coasts. The Company officials planted salad vegetables, cabbages, asparagus, cauliflowers, pumpkins, peas and beans in their factories' kitchen gardens, as Indian vegetables were not to their taste. Then fruit and vegetables from the New World started arriving, which included maize, cashew nuts, papaya, pineapple, custard apple, guava and sapodilla.

When the Mughal Empire began to break up in the eighteenth century, a rivalry developed between Delhi's declining Mughal court and Lucknow's increasingly stylish independent courtly culture. Lucknow's royal chefs made their dals and curries richer with an extravagant use of their esteemed local milk, yoghurt and cream. They refined the art of dum pukht, which had been popular since Akbar's era – a style of slow-cooking meat or rice in a container sealed with dough that's shrouded in various mythologies and manufactured stories perpetuated by chefs to this day. For instance, there are several fiercely debated tales of its origins – in Delhi, Kashmir or even South India – with some modern chefs claiming they invented the technique themselves to create a romantic folklore around their own restaurants.

Potatoes were introduced in the eighteenth century by the Portuguese or the British, either of whom probably got

them from the Dutch. They became an important ingredient in Bengali cuisine and from there spread across India. South Indian Brahmins and some other Hindu communities were suspicious of them though, as they weren't recognised by Ayurveda and were believed to cause indigestion.

It's not clear when and how tomatoes came to India, but they appear to have been introduced from Mexico or Peru in the late eighteenth century by the Portuguese, and later popularised by the British. They were initially grown for the use of Europeans, but Indians gradually started using them, Bengalis being the first to add them as a souring agent in sweet and sour curries.

In 1757 the East India Company defeated the Mughal armies and set up rule in large parts of India, still answerable to the British government. In 1833 the Company lost its trading monopoly in India; the 1857 Indian Mutiny brought an official end to the Mughal rule and marked the transfer of power to the British government; and in 1877 Queen Victoria was crowned the Empress of India, with the country officially becoming the Indian Empire.

By the nineteenth century there were thousands of East India Company administrators and army officers. The British introduced an English education system and soon well-schooled and well-travelled Indian aristocrats were living a combination of Indian and western lifestyles. They ate English and European dishes – sometimes for the sake of appearances – alongside Indian ones. The wealthy built separate kitchens to cook western meat and Indian vegetarian food. Gradually they developed a taste for western ingredients, recipes, cooking techniques and alcoholic drinks; by the twentieth century these were no longer the preserve of royalty, but also embraced by the middle classes. They remained suspicious of the 'caste-less' British who employed Muslim cooks, though, showing reluctance to share a meal with them. Perhaps just as well, as the British adaptations of Indian curries may not have been to their taste.

ANGLO-INDIAN AND
BRITISH CURRIES

THE STORY OF Anglo-Indian curries begins with the spice trade, the foundation of colonialism. Spices had been used in Europe for thousands of years. Invading Romans are said to have introduced the likes of cloves and lavender to northern Europe; but it was ginger, cinnamon, nutmeg and pepper that were the most imported spices during medieval times.

Other than lending taste and texture to a dish, a variety of mostly mythical reasons have been put forward for their use: they perked up poor people's mundane diets or the austere vegetarian food of Christian fasting days; they were exotic foods with magical characteristics; or their antibiotic properties could kill bacteria and prevent food spoilage. They were also used in medicine, perfumes, incense and embalming. They were so highly sought after that only the wealthy could afford them, and they became a status symbol.

Medieval European food was heavily influenced by Arab cookery. Arab traders controlled the spice trade, but the high prices were becoming prohibitive, leading to a need for Europeans to find a direct route. With its ideal location between east and west, the port of Venice became the centre of a thriving trade for centuries, from where spices were exported overland to the rest of Europe via the Silk Road.

Six years after Christopher Columbus's 'discovery' of the Americas, in 1498 Vasco da Gama and his crew succeeded in taking a direct sea route via the Cape of Good Hope and disembarked on the Malabar Coast to buy spices. Although their original trip was not a success, they took a lot of pepper back to sell at a massive profit. They returned for more spices and by 1530 had established headquarters in Goa in the west, along with a presence in Bengal in the east. Having defeated the Arabs they went on to dominate the spice trade in the sixteenth century, leading to a decline in business with Venice.

The English, French and Dutch had also been desperate to find their own direct routes for years. They succeeded in establishing trading posts in countries that grew spices, and by 1689 the Portuguese had lost their monopoly on the spice trade.

The British East India Company had already set up one factory in Surat in western India; now it started opening more. Presidency towns were established, which eventually became their headquarters and trading hubs, laying the foundations of British colonisation. The first was Madras in 1640, where it relocated from the region around Malabar Coast, mostly because one of the Company's chaplain's

Engraved for MILLAR's New Complete & Universal SYSTEM of GEOGRAPHY.

A PROSPECT of the Castle of SURAT, a great City of INDOSTAN, commonly called the Mogul Empire in INDIA.

mistresses lived nearby. Next was Bombay in 1661, given as a present by Charles II, who had received it as a dowry from his Portuguese wife. Finally Calcutta was chosen as the headquarters in 1690 by officials who'd been trading there for decades.

Towns and villages grew around these cities, initially in a mirror image of Britain, with shops selling European goods, bungalows, mansions, gardens, plazas, churches, taverns, army barracks, hospitals, stables, forts and cemeteries. The Company officials made a lot of money and lived a lavish, leisurely lifestyle not unlike the British aristocracy back home. They married local women and called themselves

Indian, East Indian or Anglo-Indian – a term that originally referred to the British in India, which gradually evolved to mean 'of combined European and Indian heritage' by the twentieth century.

In the early days they adopted Indian culture, ate Indian food and threw extravagant parties to show off their new social status. Their diet revolved around enormous quantities of meat – a combination of what wealthy British in Britain and rich Muslims in India would have eaten at the time, but in larger amounts.

The British invaded Goa in 1797 and remained there for seventeen years. During this time they discovered Goan

food – to their delight more meaty than that of many other regions of India, unfettered by Hindu or Muslim taboos of beef and pork. This is an important point – a lot of curries that attracted the British (and which later travelled to Britain) were prominent Muslim, Parsi or Goan Christian meat curries of the time; Hindu vegetarian food held little appeal. When they left in 1813, they took Goan cooks with them and also employed Muslim cooks.

Meanwhile in Britain in the eighteenth century curry was an antidote to British food, which had become rather plain and bland. The spicy, sweet and sour flavours of the Middle Ages had given way to French food rich in butter and sauces, and the fermented flavours inspired by Rome and Greece. French cuisine had become so influential that, like in France, spices were now reserved for cakes and puddings. Their very popularity had killed them – the more ubiquitous they'd become, the more they were dismissed as vulgar, and liable to over-stimulate wanton lusts and passions. So when curries came along and livened up the daily diet of meat and two veg, even the British with no connection to India took an interest. By the end of the century, spices had made a comeback and were considered essential.

Several recipes for mildly spiced stews had already been printed by this time, but the first published recipe in English that's specifically called curry appeared in *The Art of Cookery Made Plain and Easy* (1747) by Hannah Glasse (1708–1770). 'To make a Currey the India way' is a dish of chicken or rabbit, finely chopped onions, 'thirty peppercorns', a spoonful of rice, and coriander seeds 'browned over a fire in a clean shovel' and ground into a powder. It's simmered in water, to which butter is added after the meat has softened. In later editions, Glasse added curry powder, cayenne pepper and chopped pickles to the dish.

As British power over India grew the Company merchants became civil servants, and a few years later their interest had gone beyond commerce to acquiring territories to make even more money. Anglo-Indians didn't understand the nuances of Indian cooking, but were broadly aware that there were regional differences. They

An English Family at Table, under a Punkah or Fan, kept in motion by a Khelasy.

randomly borrowed ingredients and techniques from one part of India and added them to a dish from another. There was broad stereotyping that paid no heed to intricate differences based on location, caste, community or religion. The merchants' knowledge of using spices in Indian food was limited, so they changed and simplified recipes to suit their palate. This homogenisation led to generic pan-Indian curries that lost their regionality.

Additionally garnishes and accompaniments were taken extraordinarily seriously and included in 'curry services' – the ceremonial presenting, plating and serving of curries – though their pairing with main dishes was somewhat arbitrary. Chutneys and pickles (often made British-style with fruit and vinegar), sliced onions, desiccated coconut, 'poppadoms', peanuts, chopped cucumber and tomato, hot chilli sauce, hard-boiled eggs, grilled Bombay duck, sliced bananas (presumably a substitute for fried plantains), fried aubergine slices, potato chips and curry puffs (breaded mashed potato chops stuffed with curried meat or chicken, doused in curry sauce) were considered essential accompaniments. Some garnishes were randomly mixed into curries to 'improve' their taste. This practice lasted well into the

1980s and beyond – and there are still families across the world who cook curries this way.

Partly due to the Indian Mutiny of 1857, the East India Company was dissolved the following year. In 1877 Queen Victoria became the Empress of India, part of a wider plan by Prime Minister Disraeli to distract the working classes from poverty and instil a sense of pride in the monarchy and the empire. It worked because in Britain, a new craze started for all things Indian – not only food, but also textiles, jewellery, ornaments, paintings and furnishings. Sauces and relishes with names like Nabob's and Empress of India were launched.

There followed numerous extremely popular public exhibitions that turned India into a kind of theme park, complete with art, science, natural history, branded products and information guides, all in a funfair atmosphere surrounded by snake charmers, jugglers and dancers. There were pavilions styled like Mughal gardens, mock jungles or the Taj Mahal, with hunting trophies, silks and tea. They hosted what would today be called Indian food pop-ups, with names such as Ceylon Tea House and Curry House. An Indian waiter from one such pop-up went on to write a cookbook – not so different from today's supper-club hosts landing cookbook deals. These exhibitions marked a change in the British attitude to the colonies: rather than simply a source of luxury goods, they were seen as important trading centres for import and export.

set it in a dry warm place. Shake it regularly every day for a month when it will be ready to use.

Note.—The mango pickle may be omitted.

2244.—BENGAL RECIPE FOR MAKING MANGO CHETNEY.

Ingredients.—1½ lb. of moist sugar, ¾ lb. of salt, ¼ lb. of garlic, ¼ lb. of onions, ¾ lb. of powdered ginger, ¼ lb. of dried chilies, ¾ lb. of mustard-seed, ¾ lb. of stoned raisins, 2 bottles of best vinegar, 30 large unripe sour apples.

Mode.—The sugar must be made into syrup ; the garlic, onions and ginger be finely pounded in a mortar : the mustard-seed be washed in cold vinegar, and dried in the sun ; the apples be peeled, cored, and sliced and boiled in a bottle and a half of the vinegar. When all this is done, and the apples are quite cold, put them into a large pan, and gradually mix the whole of the rest of the ingredients, including the remaining half-bottle of vinegar. It must be well stirred until the whole is thoroughly blended,

GARLIC.

and then put into bottles for use. Tie a piece of wet bladder over the mouths of the bottles, after they are well corked. This chetney is very superior to any which can be bought, and one trial will prove it to be delicious.

Note.—This recipe was given by a native to an English lady who had long been a resident in India, and who, since her return to her native country, has become quite celebrated amongst her friends for the excellence of this Eastern relish.

Garlic. (*Fr.*—**Ail.**)—The smell of this plant is generally considered offensive, and it is the most acrimonious in its taste of the whole of the alliaceous tribe. In 1548 it was introduced into England from the shores of the Mediterranean, where it is abundant, and in Sicily it grows naturally. It was in greater repute with our ancestors than it is with ourselves, although it is still used as aseasoning herb. On the Continent, especially in Italy, it is much used, and the French consider it an essential in many made-dishes. It is generally sufficient to cut a clove of garlic and with it to rub the dish on which the substance to be flavoured is going to be served.

2245.—INDIAN CHETNEY SAUCE.

Ingredients.—8 oz. of sharp, sour apples, pared and cored, 8 oz. of tomatoes, 8 oz. of salt, 8 oz. of brown sugar, 8 oz. of stoned raisins, 4 oz. of cayenne, 4 oz. of powdered ginger, 2 oz. of garlic, 2 oz. of shalots, 3 quarts of vinegar, 1 quart of lemon-juice.

Mode.—Chop the apples in small square pieces, and add to them the other ingredients. Mix the whole well together, and put in a well-covered jar. Keep this is a warm place, and stir every day for a month, taking care to put on the lid after this operation ; strain, but do not squeeze it

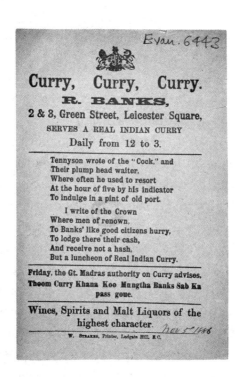

Evan. 6443

Curry, Curry, Curry.

R. BANKS,

2 & 3, Green Street, Leicester Square,

SERVES A REAL INDIAN CURRY

Daily from 12 to 3.

Tennyson wrote of the "Cock," and
Their plump head waiter,
Where often he used to resort
At the hour of five by his indicator
To indulge in a pint of old port.

I write of the Crown
Where men of renown,
To Banks' like good citizens hurry,
To lodge there their cash,
And receive not a hash,
But a luncheon of Real Indian Curry.

Friday, the Gt. Madras authority on Curry advises,
**Theom Curry Khana Koo Mungtha Banks Sab Ka
pass gone.**

**Wines, Spirits and Malt Liquors of the
highest character.** *nov 5 1886*

W. STRAKES, Printer, Ludgate Hill, E.C.

Despite never having visited India, Queen Victoria was
fascinated by the country and loved hearing about it. She
had a few Indian servants and was particularly fond of one
named Abdul Karim, who grew to be influential. Instead of
having them wait on her, she asked them to cook chicken
curries, which she loved, and ordered curries to be on the
menu of her Isle of Wight retreat, Osborne House. Her
heir Edward VII was indifferent, but her grandson George
V was so passionate about curries that he ate them almost
every lunchtime for thirty-five years, showing little interest

in any other food. Meat, game and chicken curries were prepared for him regularly, but his favourite was beefsteak with Bombay duck.

Meanwhile by the 1870s, despite the changing attitudes in Britain, curry was declining in popularity among India's new sahibs and memsahibs – younger public school-educated British bureaucrats and their naive, inexperienced wives. They regarded the old East India Company men as uncouth provincials. The racial theories of the second half of the nineteenth century meant they saw themselves as superior, and their role as harbingers of civilisation in what they considered a backward country. Brisk and efficient, they weren't there to get rich quick like their laid-back predecessors. They criticised Indian food as being 'inordinately greasy and sweet' and 'quite unsuited to European taste'.[7]

French and English cookery was now preferred to curry, which was consigned to breakfast or lunch, or served mostly at clubs and army barracks, or on camping trips or long travels. Curries disappeared from the more formal and prestigious dinner menus. All this was in keeping with the prevalent trends in the Britain they had left behind, though these were now changing back home. New cookbooks appeared instructing the memsahibs on 'how best to produce, under the special circumstances of the country, the dishes approved by the taste of polite society at home'.[8]

This led to the cobbling together of bland pseudo-European dishes – usually from hard-to-find, inferior tinned

ingredients (canning technology was in its early stages). The Suez Canal had opened, which made it easier to ship European goods to India. Indian cooks, who were unfamiliar with the equipment, techniques and recipes, muddled through them, bringing their own touches such as adding spices to roast meats and turning casseroles into curries.

Although Anglo-Indian curries had been out of favour gentlemen's clubs still served them eagerly. These clubs had been increasing in number since the Bengal Club was established in Calcutta in 1827, the Byculla Club in Bombay in 1833 and the Madras Club in Madras in the same year. They all became famous for their curries, which were sold to golfers and their wives for weekend club lunches labelled 'mild', 'medium' and 'hot' – a practice later taken up by Britain's Indian restaurateurs.

Curries served on the P&O Ferries between England and India provided a good introduction to Indian food; they were also eaten in the army messes. During the Second World War, army cooks were given monthly supplies of curry powder and shown how to make curries using raisins, tropical fruit and a roux made of curry powder and plain flour. Many British men who'd never eaten a curry before got their first taste in the army or navy.

The most famous of all British army officers in India was Arthur Kenney-Herbert (1840–1916), who wrote under the pseudonym Wyvern. Hugely fond of Indian food, he was a major curry influencer of his day. His *Culinary Jottings for*

October 24th November 1st

Madras (1878) was the best-known and most authoritative piece of work on Indian food by an English writer at that time, and has a renowned chapter on curry.

Indian cookbooks aimed at Anglo-Indians started appearing during the nineteenth century, and there were entire sections on curry in two of the most influential and plagiarised cookbooks of the time: *Modern Cookery for Private Families* (1845) by Eliza Acton (1799–1859), and the later editions of *Mrs Beeton's Book of Household Management* (first published in 1861) by Isabella Beeton (1836–1855).

The entrepreneur Mrs Agnes B. Marshall (1855–1905), always one step ahead of everyone else in Victorian and Edwardian England, sold own-label curry powders; in her *Mrs A. B. Marshall's Cookery Book* (1888) she gave elaborate curry recipes with pretentious French names like 'curried

INDIAN COOKS.

CHAPTER LI.

GENERAL OBSERVATIONS ON INDIAN COOKERY.

2865. *Housekeeping in India* is an utterly different thing to house-keeping here. The mistress cannot undertake the personal supervision of her kitchen, which is not in the house or bungalow, but outside, and very likely some distance away. She will also soon learn (that is supposing she has been accustomed to English housekeeping) that it is impossible to treat Indian servants in the same manner as those on whom she has been accustomed to depend for daily service. Indian servants are good, many of them, but they cannot be trusted implicitly, and *will* cheat if they have a chance, and it is absolutely necessary to look after the cook (*Khánsámán*), who will probably be the marketer.

It is best to give him his orders over night, that he may go early to the bazaar to buy. There is a tariff of all articles sold at the bazaar, regulated by the bazaar master and Cantonment Magistrate, therefore having mastered the value of the various coins and a few words for every day wants in the way of food, it should be difficult for your *Khánsámán* to exercise his proclivities for defrauding you.

Drink is the greatest expense in housekeeping. The climate is a thirsty one and the water is bad, so filled with animalculæ that it cannot be drank with pheasant à la Pondicherry' and 'curried lobsters à la sultan'. There were also all-Indian cookbooks such as *Indian Cookery* (1861) by Richard Terry, the chef at London's Oriental Club. Daniel Santiagoe, an Indian cook and former domestic servant, wrote the well-received *Curry Cook's Assistant: Curries and How to Make Them in England in the Original Style* (1889).

Not everyone enjoyed curry though; many preferred traditional British fare. Curries initially had an image problem. The ideal method of cooking meat was thought to be roasting, boiling or baking; only the lower classes chopped up leftovers and cooked them in a stew, which curries in the early days were categorised as. It was only during the rise of the middle classes in the first half of the nineteenth century that changing attitudes towards running economical households made curries acceptable. A housewife on a tight budget using up cold meat was admired for being thrifty. In *Mrs Beeton's Book of Household Management*, aimed at the middle classes, she categorised curries as 'cold meat cookery'.

By the second half of the nineteenth century, British views were evolving further, and curry was embraced for its practicality and perceived health benefits. Former memsahibs, who had rejected curry so disdainfully while in India, suddenly set themselves up as experts.

Selim's True India Curries was among the first packaged brand, making its debut at the Lord Mayor's Banquet in

AN EXQUISITE AND DELICATELY FLAVOURED CURRY.

MRS A.B.MARSHALL'S

CURRY POWDER

A Curry of Exquisite Flavor, of the kind prevalent in the MADRAS PRESIDENCY.

30 & 32 MORTIMER STREET. LONDON.W.

Per bottle, 6d., 1s., and 2s. This Label on each bottle.

1842. It was an instant hit, widely used by caterers and pub chefs and endorsed by cookery writers such as Eliza Acton. Ex-army officer Edmund White, the founder of Selim's, claimed that the heat of his curry paste could aid digestion by stimulating the stomach, improving blood circulation and keeping the mind sharp. Although the idea that curries were healthy had been around for years, such exaggerated claims misfired and led to scepticism. However the advertising must have worked: so popular were Selim's curry pastes that they were available in Army & Navy stores until the 1930s.

British curries were now made from everything – ranging from cheap cuts of meat, calves' feet and sheep's heads, to lobsters and oysters. As French influence continued, leading to the serving of meals in courses, curries became more elegant. No longer only about using up leftovers, they started appearing at smart dinner parties. The anonymous author of *Modern Domestic Cookery* (1852), known simply as 'A Lady', wrote that while curry was 'formerly a dish almost exclusively for the tables of those who had made a long residence in India, (it) is now so completely naturalised, that few dinners are thought complete unless one is on the table'.

Eliza Acton advocated the use of 'tamarinds imported in the shell – not preserved'.[9] They may not have been widely available, though, as lemon juice, gooseberries or verjuice were used as substitutes to give a sour flavour. Other stand-ins included apples for mangoes, cucumber for bitter gourd, and redcurrant or other fruit jam for jaggery. Over time, these ceased being replacement ingredients and were considered essential to a good curry. By the end of the century the super-hot curries of previous years had become unfashionable, and the amount of chilli was reducing. Subtle spicing was considered more refined.

There were minor differences in the way Anglo-Indians in India and the British in Britain prepared curries, but the formula was broadly the same: meat and onions (and sometimes curry paste) were fried in butter, then curry powder and stock or milk were added, the curry was simmered for a long time and then finished with lemon juice and cream. How the lemon didn't curdle the cream and turn it into paneer is a mystery I haven't solved.

This Anglo-Indian template could be turned into a 'Bengal chicken curry', a 'Malay prawn curry with coconut' and so on. This cooking-by-numbers formula was later adopted by Bengali seamen – some of whom had worked for Anglo-Indians – in Britain's early Indian restaurants.

After curry's popularity peaked during the Victorian era, it was looked down on rather snobbishly as 'spicy and disagreeable to respectable middle-class English stomachs'.[10] By the 1950s, the middle classes were offended by their smell, and housewives just put a pinch of curry powder in their stews instead of making an actual curry. On the few occasions they did make it, it was served in the centre of, or around, a ring of white rice – but more usually, just eaten with potatoes and boiled vegetables.

Today the huge impact that Anglo-Indian ingredients, techniques and recipes have had on Indian cooking is clear to see – from the ubiquitous British-grown 'mixed vegetables' combo of carrots, green beans, peas, cauliflower and potatoes found in hundreds of pulaos and 'Mughlai' curries, to a variety of breaded chops and cutlets. Many British dishes have been Indianised and thoroughly incorporated into the local cuisines, especially in Kolkata and Mumbai, and continue to be served in homes, clubs and hotel restaurants.

CURRY POWDER

ONE OF THE MAJOR differences between curries in India and curries in Britain was the use of curry powder, which nobody in India would have used up until the twentieth century. Here we're talking specifically about the generic spice mix labelled as 'curry powder', not regional Indian spice blends like Pondicherry vadouvan masala, Kashmiri ver masala or East Indian bottle masala. In India, spices were freshly ground on grinding stones every day, with wealthy families employing an assistant specifically to do this job.

In Britain in the eighteenth century the returned Anglo-Indians initially bought individual spices from the chemist; there's no mention of curry powders in the early cook-books. Then, as their familiarity with Indian cuisine grew, they started thinking of curries as variations on one stand-ard stew-like theme and began making recipes for spice mixes to which they gave the umbrella term 'curry powder'.

Cookery writers of the day encouraged its use. Arthur Kenney-Herbert insisted that it was better to make curry

GENUINE
CURRIE POWDER.

This preparation is greatly superior to those generally sold, being prepared from an Original Recipe, and with the finest and choicest ingredients.

TO PREPARE A CURRIE.

Cut the Fowl, Rabbit, or Meat into small pieces, and fry them in butter with a sliced onion; then stew them for twenty minutes in a sufficient quantity of beef gravy or water, adding two or three large spoonfuls of the Currie Powder, two ounces of butter, and the juice of a lemon, for the weight of a large Fowl.

PREPARED BY

PROSSER, PHARMACEUTICAL CHEMIST,

By Appointment to the Garrison,

7, HEAD STREET, COLCHESTER.

powder to ensure consistency of taste instead of relying on spices ground by an inexperienced native cook who might come up with their own concoctions. He incorrectly claimed that these powders improved with age and should be made and stored in large quantities. (This would actually make spices go rancid.) He approved of high-quality ready-made brands like Barrie's Madras curry powder, but not inferior ones padded out with cornflour. Mrs Beeton, too, advised buying good curry powders rather than making them at home, suggesting they tasted better and were more economical. Curry powders were indeed inexpensive and gave a predictably consistent taste for those who found traditional Indian food too hot and pungent. However, some of these writers were only trying to promote their own-label brands.

The early curry powders were broadly based on various spice mixes of South India such as sambar and rasam powders – the origins of Madras curry powder central to Madras curries. There were also Bengal and Bombay curry powders, which appear to have become extinct, based vaguely on spice blends from those regions.

Sorlie's Perfumery Warehouse in London's Piccadilly had been advertising curry powder as early as 1784; by the 1840s, Indian products were becoming widely available. A decade later, curry powder – initially home-made, then commercially available – was so common that it was used in most British curries. Ten years later, curry pastes like the Empress brand were sold in Fortnum & Mason, Halls of London and a Crosse & Blackwell shop in London's Soho. Imports of turmeric tripled during the nineteenth century – which shows that the popular yellow spice was trendy long before turmeric lattes came along.

By the end of the nineteenth century curry powders in mild, medium and hot varieties were commonly found even in ordinary grocery stores. The over-reliance on them, however, meant that all British curries tasted the same.

Today the use of ready-made curry powders and pastes in Indian dishes in Britain has declined (though they're still used in non-Indian recipes) as more people are keen to learn how to cook 'authentic' food. Recipes that once listed Madras curry powder now suggest using garam masala instead.

In India, many families continue to hire speciality masala makers famed for their signature spice blends to make a few weeks' supply. In many communities, women still get together to grind spices using large pestles and mortars – though most just use coffee grinders.

Equally, though, in India the use of every type of packaged masala mix has skyrocketed to an astonishing degree in the last twenty years – not so much curry powder, which a few Indians do occasionally use, but bespoke blends aimed at cooking specific dishes like Kolhapuri chicken curry or Mangalore fish fry.

HOW CURRY CAME
TO BRITAIN

ACCORDING TO BOTH anecdotal and national news reports, a couple of curry-related questions have appeared in recent British citizenship tests, more formally known as the Life in the UK test.[11] One referred to a famous 2001 speech by the former UK Foreign Secretary Robin Cook (1946–2005) in which he said:

> Chicken tikka masala is now a true British national dish, not only because it is the most popular, but because it is a perfect illustration of the way Britain absorbs and adapts external influences. Chicken tikka is an Indian dish. The masala sauce was added to satisfy the desire of British people to have their meat served in gravy.

His naively optimistic but flawed championing of multi-culturalism comes up in every single discourse about curry. My local Persian grocer told me he passed his test because he knew the answer to the question of 'true British national dish' was 'chicken tikka masala', whereas his friend, who

replied 'fish and chips', failed. Later there was another question on when Sake Dean Mahomed opened the first curry house in the UK. I find it astonishing that would-be British citizens are expected to know this kind of curry history trivia.

Whether you're taking a citizenship test or not, you might like to know that the answer is 1810. The restaurant was called Hindoostane Coffee House, and the Indian-born entrepreneur and former army officer Mahomed (1759–1851) opened it at 34 George Street in Marylebone (now renumbered 102). Its handwritten menu of over twenty-five dishes such as chicken curry, lobster curry and 'coolmah' (presumably korma) of lamb or veal fetched £8,500 at an auction in London in 2018.

Its raj-themed furniture consisted of bamboo cane chairs and Indian ornaments, and there was a separate smoking room with hookah pipes. It was aimed at wealthy retired Anglo-Indian East India Company officials who had settled nearby, first in Portman Square and Regent's Park, then Bayswater and South Kensington.

These returned Anglo-Indians were known as nabobs, an anglicised version of the Indian word *nawab*, meaning district governor. They tried to recreate their life in India, employing Indian cooks and eating curries in coffee houses. Despite a favourable review by Ralph Rylance in London's first restaurant guide *The Epicure's Almanack: Eating & Drinking in Regency London* in 1815 (republished by the British Library in 2012), the restaurant closed after a year as it wasn't making enough money. One reason could be that the nabobs had already brought back cooks, maids or former memsahibs from India to make curries at home.

Additionally there were more established coffee houses closer to the City of London where the nabobs had been congregating for far longer. Norris Street Coffee House on Haymarket had already been selling curries and curry pastes since 1773, if not earlier, and even did home deliveries in what must have been London's first Indian delivery service. There was also the popular Jerusalem Coffee House in Cornhill, whose owner was said to have been cured of an ailment with curry powder when all medicines had failed. Another much-loved venue was the Oriental Club, which opened in 1824. After serving French food for its first fifteen years, it started selling Indian dishes. It's still open today, but is strictly a private members' club and serves curries in its restaurant and bar to its members.

The next to open were restaurants by Bangladeshi lascars, an anglicised word for sailors. Although Bangladeshi is now technically correct, Bangladesh, like Pakistan, was once part of India. When Pakistan was forced to separate from India during the Partition of 1947, what was then known as East Bengal became East Pakistan, then was separated from Pakistan after the Indo-Pakistani War of 1971 and became Bangladesh. Until then everyone was Indian. Today, although there are regional differences in food, there are many similarities between countries due to the shared history.

The majority of these lascars had come from a sailors' community central to a small district called Sylhet, a largely Muslim region with jungles and tea plantations on the northeastern border with Assam. Its many waterways that connected Assam's tea gardens with Calcutta's port made it a prime location. In the 1840s the British started running steamships in these waterways and employed cheap, hard-working Sylheti boatmen, who later found jobs in steamships travelling abroad.

They weren't educated and couldn't speak English, so couldn't get more desirable jobs as deckhands. They ended

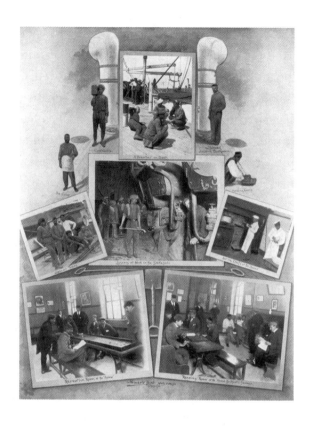

up working in noisy engine rooms, which were so hot due to coal fires and so dangerous because of exploding boilers that many tragically died. The ones who survived were extremely poorly paid and, unsurprisingly, jumped ship to settle in Rangoon, Singapore, Southampton, New York or London.

There were downmarket boarding houses in White-chapel and the 'Oriental Quarter' of Shadwell High Street, where the lascars stayed while waiting to embark their ships. Some, owned by earlier seamen, doubled as gambling and opium dens fronted by the seamen's English wives and mistresses. By the early twentieth century the conditions at these boarding houses had improved. One of the best known was located on the Victoria Dock Road, run by a Bengali named Mr Ali. He owned a small coffee shop nearby where the Sylheti sailors bought curry and rice – this must have been London's first Bangladeshi restaurant.

Others copied him, and by the 1940s there were several Sylheti-owned boarding houses and cafés at Sandy Row, Brick Lane, New Road and Commercial Road. They largely catered to the culinary and social needs of lascars leaving or returning to the area. It was difficult for the deserters to find work, so many made a living from begging, stealing, sweeping streets and churchyards or selling cheap goods such as chocolate, coffee and curry powder. Others found jobs as cooks in the nabobs' households. Most found employment in catering as cleaners, kitchen porters or washers-up in restaurants, clubs and hotels, including Veeraswamy's.

Veeraswamy, as it's now known (the 's has been dropped) is today believed to be Britain's oldest surviving Indian restaurant. It started as a pop-up café at the hugely popular British Empire Exhibition in Wembley in 1924–5, which had millions of visitors. There was an Indian section in a mock-Taj Mahal pavilion, run by an entrepreneur named Edward Palmer, who came from an Anglo-Indian banking dynasty. His great-grandfather William Palmer was an English military officer married to a Hyderabadi princess

– the name Veeraswamy is said to have been taken from her side of the family. He sold curries, pulaos and tea, and wrote an influential cookbook. He was the founder of E. P. Veeraswamy & Co. Indian Food Specialists, which imported spices, curry pastes and chutneys from India and sold them under the brand name Nizam.

After the massive success of his pop-up, Palmer opened a permanent restaurant the following year in Regent Street. In the early days, it had a similar raj theme as his temporary venue, barely changed from the Hindoostane Coffee House days, with cane chairs, potted palms, high ceilings, lights from the Maharaja of Mysore's palace and waiters in Indian bearers' uniforms. (Even today a turbaned doorman can be found at the entrance.) It served duck vindaloo, Madras curry and dopiaza, alongside an English menu of rump steak and lamb cutlets. Customers included celebrities, politicians and royalty. Today only a couple of dishes survive from the original menu, of which the mulligatawny, made to the original recipe, is exquisite.

Although Veeraswamy's was pioneering, there were many others. One was Abdullah's in Soho's Old Compton Street in the 1920s, run by 'an expert cook ... from Bombay', who delivered to Buckingham Palace and came highly recommended by the Indian Secretary of State. There were also Salut e Hind in Holborn in 1911; Ayub Ali Master's Curry Café in Commercial Street in the 1920s; Dilkush in Windmill Street, taken over by Shah Abdul Majid Qureshi

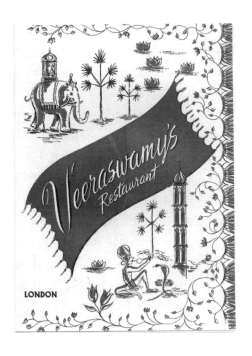

in 1938, said to be the first Sylheti-owned restaurant in the West End; Anglo-Asian, which was opened by Mosrof Ali and Israel Miah in Knightsbridge in 1942; and Southall's first Punjabi restaurant in 1958. Others included India Burma in Leicester Square and Khayam off Tottenham Court Road.

Two of the most significant venues catered for Indian students. The first was Shafi's on Gerrard Street, which was hugely popular. It was set up in 1920 by Yassim and Rahim Mohammed from North India, who had come to Britain as students and saw a gap in the market. The brothers provided a friendly ear to their homesick customers. Another was Kohinoor in the West End's Roper Street, established in the 1920s by another former student, Bir Bahadur. He was so successful that he brought his brothers over from Delhi and turned it into a nationwide chain by the late 1940s – the Dishoom of its day.

Other than students early customers were ageing nabobs or young British men who'd been posted to India during the war and had developed a taste for curry in the army. Working conditions were often poor and the pay was low, but the Sylheti seamen put up with these in order to save enough money to buy their own places, keeping their head down and serving with a mixture of resignation and gentle defiance. Kohinoor treated them well and provided training to nearly all first-generation Bangladeshis, including Veeraswamy's staff, in cooking, food presentation, management and business skills.

The early décor – which remained unchanged well into the 1990s – mimicked raj-era clubs with their swirly patterned red-and-gold flock wallpaper, heavy carved wooden furniture, brightly coloured tablecloths and brass ornaments: a budget version of the Veeraswamy look.

By the end of the Second World War many bomb-damaged cafés and fish and chip shops lay derelict, so the lascars started buying them up and turned them into small restaurants. Initially the customers were mostly white working-class men; at first, the owners didn't change the

restaurants' names or menus as they didn't want to alienate them, only adding rice and curry to the existing lists of tea, coffee, pies and fish and chips. Eventually they started adopting Anglo-Indian names, then opening late to catch the post-pub trade as the former chip shops had done. Unfortunately this meant having to deal with drunk, rowdy customers – which continues to be a big problem in parts of Britain to this day.

Gradually the customers became more adventurous and started ordering curry to eat as a sauce for their chips, which is how the tradition of chips with curry sauce was born. Today, according to a UK survey,[12] curry sauce – a thick yellow-ish gravy made from curry powder – is the third most popular topping for chips after ketchup and mushy peas.

One customer must have discovered that a hot vindaloo was an effective counterpoint to a night of beer drinking, which reinforced the idea of going for a curry after the pub.[13] This then led to a lot of macho posturing, with young men daring each other to eat the hottest possible curries. As curry became accepted, British dishes were dropped altogether, and the venues became fully Indian.

The early restaurants in Britain copied their menus from Veeraswamy's, Shafi's and Kohinoor – which served the kind of food that the few restaurants that existed in North India at the time sold. These in turn were based on what Anglo-Indians liked to eat.

These restaurants had to interpret, cook and serve a highly complex cuisine promptly to impatient customers. There were many inexperienced cooks who didn't have time for grinding spices, traditional slow-cooking and the layering of flavours in stages, so they created shortcuts. Moreover, customers' palates were still conservative, and many of them hated garlic, coriander and chillies. So they used quick-fix tricks like adding boiled onion paste to thicken curries, which gave them a raw taste, or a few handy spices to pep up wholesale jars of curry pastes and sauces. To make Madras curry, they would add a lot of chillies; for korma, cream and ground almonds, and so on. Gradually each type of curry was reduced to its overriding character-istic – so Madras was simply 'hot' and korma was 'mild'.

According to industry insiders and suppliers of branded curry sauces, many restaurant curries continue to be made in this way today, and in fact some customers prefer the predictability of standardisation. Now criticised for being 'inauthentic', these shortcuts were nonetheless deemed necessary commercial considerations at the time. Some argue that instead of comparing these curry-house curries with home-made ones, they should be regarded as a sepa-rate genre in their own right. In recent years young diaspora Indians, who grew up eating them, have celebrated them as ingenious products of pioneering immigrants.

In the 1960s Britain prospered with industrialisa-tion, while poverty in the newly formed Asian countries meant that Asians were often forced to take up badly paid jobs abroad. There was a lot of work available so immi-gration was encouraged in the late 1950s. Bangladeshis could now get British passports and bring their families over. White labourers didn't want to work in the growing food-processing, plastics, synthetic textile and rubber industries in West London, so the companies advertised in newspapers in India, and by the 1960s a large number of Indians had settled in Southall. The same happened with the clothing industry in Tower Hamlets.

This pattern continued in Manchester and Bradford in the north of England, too – white male workers dismissed night shifts in textile factories as women's work, so Pakistanis from Punjab took those jobs and later went on to open restaurants. There were also Punjabi Muslim, Sikh and Gujarati immigrants, many of whom had been kicked out of Idi Amin's Uganda and Kenya in the early 1970s, who took jobs in metal and car factories in Birmingham. Areas with large Indian populations such as Bradford and Leicester, plus London's Brick Lane, Southall and Wembley, expanded and their restaurants were promoted as tourist destinations by the local councils. The most famous are Birmingham's Balti Triangle, Manchester's Curry Mile and Brick Lane's Bangla Town.

In the 1970s many curry houses became 'tandoori' restaurants, even the ones that didn't necessarily own a tandoor oven. They were copying the smart, ground-breaking Moti Mahal in Delhi, opened in 1948 by a Pakistani refugee named Kundan Lal Gujaral. He had installed a clay oven to make tandoori chicken, naans and kababs. In Britain, it was either Veeraswamy's or Gaylord that imported the first tandoor in the early 1960s.

After this came balti houses in the 1980s. Balti curries are made by stir-frying pre-cooked marinated meat in a toma-to-onion gravy. This form of cooking is believed to have been created by Pakistani restaurateurs in Birmingham, based on the food of Baltistan, a province in Pakistan near the Himalayas. It bears no similarity to the food of that region, though, so it's a bit baffling. Balti also means 'bucket' in Hindi, so another theory is that it refers to the bucket-like pans with two handles that the dishes are served in.

In 1982 London's first Modern Indian restaurant, Bombay Brasserie, opened in South Kensington to celebrate 'real Indian food' with the aim of changing the perception of Indian restaurants as cheap and downmarket. 'Modern Indian' – with a capital 'M' – refers to restaurants that are not only smart and contemporary in their look and decor, but also thoroughly current in terms of the menu and planning that goes into each dish. They might showcase a rare regional speciality from fifty years ago, an unusual ingredient or a witty interpretation of a dish the chef enjoyed in their childhood; the owners and cooks are well educated and widely travelled. They grind their own masalas and make each element of the dish – sauce, garnish, chutney – from scratch. Reputation and recognition are hugely important to them.

Growing up in the 1980s I remember the buzz around Bombay Brasserie – newspaper reports showed a glamorous conservatory filled with plants and chic pink tablecloths, and my parents were excited that one of the Brasserie's most famous customers, Tom Cruise, 'would now know what proper Indian food tastes like'. Bombay Brasserie is still around, but no longer as prominent. Many more Modern Indians have followed and today Britain's – particularly London's – Indian dining scene has changed beyond recognition. These glamorous venues cater for a different clientele altogether: trendy young Indian professionals, wealthy tourists, affluent families and Mumbai's billionaires who rent apartments in Mayfair, dividing their time between India and the UK.

They also reflect changes in immigration patterns. Along with other less expensive but attractively designed mid-price restaurants, they're typically owned by second- or third-generation Indians, and reflect a modern, confident India that's been stepping out of its colonial shadows. Many even combine raj nostalgia with spinning a story, whether it's 'authentic food', 'regional dishes', 'family recipes handed down the generations' or an 'exciting new concept'.

Meanwhile, the old-school curry houses are in decline or disrepair. The children of the restaurateurs, educated and secure in white-collar jobs, no longer want to work in an industry with long hours, low pay and often rude or racist customers. In India, Pakistan and Bangladesh, they might also be mocked for doing work that carries little prestige. The number of Brick Lane curry houses has reduced from sixty-six in its heyday to twenty-three in 2021; on the other hand a few cafés serving delicious lesser-known, traditional Bangladeshi fare have opened in the area and are thriving.

Perhaps 2001 shouldn't be remembered for Robin Cook's speech; it should rather be marked as being the year in which two Indian restaurants in the UK became the first to gain Michelin stars. Chicken tikka masala was already on its way out.

POPULAR INDIAN RESTAURANT CURRIES

AMONG THE MOST popular restaurant curries in India are chana masala, dum aloo, sag paneer, Kerala fish curry, mirchi ka salan, murgh mussallam, vegetable makhanwala, vegetable kolhapuri, chicken xacuti, navratna korma, avial and sorpotel, to mention just a few. In British restaurants, these are either relegated to the 'side dishes' section, especially if they're vegetarian, or not found at all.

Here's a look at the most popular Mughlai-Anglo Indian-Bangladeshi restaurant curries found in Britain and around the world.

KORMA

This is a Persian-influenced Mughlai Muslim curry of yoghurt-marinated meat that's browned and then gently cooked over a low heat in a sealed pot. The name refers to the braising technique. The original Mughlai recipe involved cooking lamb or chicken pieces with onions, ginger, garlic and spices in a ground-almond gravy, but after the Mughlai influence had diminished and the Lucknow court became more influential, a lot of cream was added to make it rich.

Anglo-Indians then simplified it, using less ghee, yoghurt and spices and no cream, turning it into a generic, slightly sweet curry. In British restaurants, korma means any mild, creamy curry with yoghurt, cream, or cashew or almond paste.

Korma was once dismissed by the English memsahib Flora Annie Steel (1847–1949) as 'one of the richest of Hindoostani curries ... but quite unsuited to European taste'.[14] European tastes must have changed because it's currently Britain's number-one favourite Indian curry.

TIKKA MASALA

Yoghurt- and spice-marinated chicken pieces are grilled or baked in a tandoor or an oven, then cooked in a creamy tomato-onion gravy coloured bright red with Kashmiri chillies, paprika or food colouring.

According to an oft-repeated legend – and possibly an urban myth – chicken tikka masala was created by the Glasgow restaurateur Ali Ahmed Aslam of Shish Mahal, who added a tin of tomato soup and cream to chicken tikka – a kabab of spiced, marinated, tandoor-cooked chicken pieces – because a customer complained that it was too dry. The British were used to eating curry sauce with their kababs;

moreover, they associated Indian food only with curry, so a dry kabab was not acceptable. The customer loved the dish so much he told his friends and a legend was born.

Another theory is that Delhi's Moti Mahal restaurant invented tandoori chicken, and to appeal to people who demanded a richer dish – and supposedly also to use up leftovers – the chef cooked it in a tomato, cream and butter sauce, making it the forerunner of tikka masala.

Others have speculated that it's a curry-house version of butter chicken, or similar curries found in Punjab in the 1970s. Yet another story is that it's an adaptation of a recipe for Mughlai-style shahi chicken masala in Mrs Balbir Singh's influential 1961 cookbook *Indian Cookery*, made from cream, yoghurt and khoya (thickened dehydrated milk).

VINDALOO

This is the best-known Goan curry outside India, though I'm told not so popular in Goa itself. The Portuguese in the eighteenth century taught their Christian converts how to cook pork dishes, the best-loved of which was *carne de vinha d'alhos* (meat preserved by Portuguese sailors in barrels of red wine, wine vinegar and garlic). The Goans adapted it into a hot, sour curry which combined the Portuguese love of tangy flavours of meat in vinegar with South Indian tamarind and black pepper, using local coconut toddy vinegar made by Franciscan priests. To this they later added cinnamon, cloves and the newly discovered hot red chillies that the Portuguese had become very fond of and used in abundance.

The curry was also made with chicken or duck – the latter being particularly beloved of Anglo-Indians. A more contemporary British-Bangladeshi invention is tindaloo, made with even more chillies.

MADRAS

Madras curry is not eaten in Madras, which is not even called Madras any more. It's a very hot curry with a tomato-onion gravy flavoured with Madras curry powder. Broadly based on South Indian spice mixes, it originally contained dried red chillies, curry leaves and legumes like urad or chana dal, which are often used as spices in South India.

Anglo-Indians classified their curries into three main styles, based vaguely on the regional differences of their presidency towns as Madras, Bombay and Bengal curries. They took one or two distinctive aspects of a region's style and applied them indiscriminately to each type of curry. So, for instance, as South Indian food is usually hotter than that of other regions, all hot curries were named Madras. Somehow Bombay curries were ones that were served with Bombay duck and *papads* ('poppadoms'), and Bengal curries were made from fish or vegetables. Bombay and Bengal seem to have largely disappeared, but Madras is still very much in demand.

Daniel Santiagoe gave a recipe for beef Madras in his cookbook *The Curry Cook's Assistant; or Curries, How to Make them in England in their Original Style* (1889). He claimed Madras was superior to Bengal or Bombay curry, and that it was customary for the wealthy in Madras to employ a *thanney kareyitchi* – a woman whose only job was to chop vegetables and make curries. He wrote that Madras was the only city where you could find a proper curry (plus Ceylon – the former name for Sri Lanka – where cooks from Madras had moved years ago). He also suggested that although Madras could be made with or without coconut, tamarind was essential as it gave a better flavour than lemon juice, along with vinegar and curry leaves.

Many Anglo-Indians like Kenney-Herbert extolled the virtues of curry-making in Madras, lamenting that it was now a lost art as the old cooks had died and the recipes had not been recorded. The writer and educator C. Herman Senn (1862–1934) claimed that Madras 'is of the purest and the best classical period – the high old curry made perfect'.[15] In British restaurants, Madras is shorthand for any very hot curry.

JALFREZI

This is a curry of Bengali origin in which meat, fish, paneer or vegetables are stir-fried with onions, tomatoes, green chillies and green bell peppers, using the stir-frying technique introduced to India by Chinese immigrants.

Anglo-Indians cooked it to use up leftover cold roast meat or chicken.

DOPIAZA

The word *dopiaza* means 'two onions'. Some have suggested that it refers to two types of onions used in this Persian-influenced slow-cooked meat curry; or that onions are used in two different forms, like sliced and pulped; or that onions are added at two different stages of cooking. However in *Ain I Akbari* there are two onions listed compared to one used elsewhere – so it's fair to say that one traditional meaning is 'twice the amount of onion used'. It can be made from lamb, mutton, beef, chicken, shrimp or okra, and soured using fresh green mangoes, dried green mango powder (*amchoor*) or lemon juice.

The British traveller Reverend Samuel Purchas, who visited India in the seventeenth century, singled out dopiaza for praise in *Purchas, His Pilgrim*: 'Among many dishes … I will take notice but of one they call … dopiaza, made of venison cut in slices, to which they put onions and herbs, some roots, with a little spice and butter: the most savoury meat I ever tasted.'

ROGAN JOSH

This is a Kashmiri curry of yoghurt-marinated lamb, mutton or goat. Its distinctive red colour once came from two different flowers, but nowadays mild Kashmiri red chilli powder or food colouring (natural or artificial) is more likely to be used. It's possibly of Persian origin, brought to Kashmir by the Mughals, but there are many complicated and contradictory theories as to its origins.

There are a few different variations. Kashmiri Brahmins add yoghurt, fennel seeds and asafoetida, and Muslim cooks use a lot of onions and garlic. The original Kashmiri version doesn't contain tomatoes, but in curry houses you're more likely to find it cooked Punjabi-style with the addition of tomatoes.

DHANSAK

This is a Persian-Gujarati sweet-and-sour stew from the Parsi community, made from mutton, goat or chicken and mixed pulses like split pigeon peas, split moong beans, Bengal gram, red lentils and brown lentils, combined with vegetables like aubergines, pumpkin and fenugreek leaves. It's flavoured with dhansak masala, jaggery, tamarind and mint leaves, and eaten with 'brown' (caramelised onion) rice.

East India Company officials learned to make it from Parsis, who worked in shipping and were later employed as butlers. In curry houses it's usually a simpler dish of red lentils, chicken or lamb, spinach and tamarind or pineapple.

PASANDA

This is a subtly spiced curry of yoghurt-marinated lamb, chicken, goat, beef or king prawn pieces flavoured with cardamom and black pepper in an onion-based gravy. The word means 'favourite' in several Indian languages and refers to the cut of meat that's sliced into long strips and flattened. A curry similar to pasanda already existed in India when it was adapted by Mughlai cooks. In curry houses it's usually a generic mild curry enriched with coconut milk, yoghurt, cream or ground almonds.

PHALL

This is the hottest of all British-Bangladeshi curries, said to have been invented in Birmingham, with lamb or chicken cooked in a tomato gravy flavoured with ginger and fennel seeds. *Phal* means 'fruit' in Hindi, but as there are no fruity ingredients its name is puzzling. It's unrelated to *phaal* from Bangalore, which is a different type of curry altogether.

TIPS FOR MAKING A GOOD CURRY

Choose your fat according to which region the curry is from as it will make a real difference to the taste of the finished dish – for instance, Bengalis and Punjabis often use mustard oil, South Indians cook with coconut oil and so on. Use ghee if you're aiming for a richer mouthfeel.

Be careful not to burn whole spices when tempering, otherwise your curry will taste bitter. Remove the pan from the heat before adding asafoetida as it's the quickest to burn.

Gently sauté finely minced onions for a minimum of ten to fifteen minutes, preferably longer, then add ginger and garlic, chopped tomatoes and ground spices. Cook until the fat floats to the surface and the mixture leaves the side of the pan. This is the key to a good North Indian curry, otherwise it will taste raw.

If using yoghurt, whip it thoroughly and pour it in bit by bit over a gentle heat, stirring continuously to avoid curdling.

CURRIES AROUND
THE WORLD

OF COURSE CURRIES are not only found in India and Britain; most other countries have curry or curry-like dishes too. There were several ways in which curry spread around the world, but the most significant was through Indian indentured labourers.

Slavery was abolished in the British Empire in 1833 and, unsurprisingly, the former slaves didn't want to return to do back-breaking plantation work. So the British government decided that the shortfall of tea, coffee, sugar and palm-oil plantation workers could be made up by Indian labourers. They introduced a system not dissimilar to slavery in which poor, largely Hindu peasants signed binding contracts to work for five, seven or ten years.

In return they were given food, housing, clothes and medicine and were paid minimum wages. They received free entry to whichever country required their services, and had a choice between returning for free or staying there and owning free land. Many labourers were from poverty-stricken families so most chose the latter option.

The first workers were shipped to Demerara in 1838; then Mauritius from 1843; British Guyana, Trinidad and Jamaica from 1845; South Africa and Fiji from the 1870s, and some went to Ceylon and Malaysia. They cooked their family recipes, adapting them using native ingredients, thereby changing the countries' own culinary traditions.

In addition the British also introduced curry to their colonies by exporting curry powders, curry pastes and curry cookbooks. Anglo-Indian officials who went to live or work abroad also took their own recipes.

What follows is a broad and generalised overview of popular curries around the world; there are many regional variations and other intricate details about each type of curry that are too numerous to list here.

INDONESIA, MALAYSIA, SINGAPORE

As in many Asian countries rice is the main dish, served with several accompaniments that include curries. They're often made by frying a paste of onions or shallots, chillies, aromatics like galangal, fresh herbs and whole or ground spices first. Other ingredients can include lemongrass, makrut lime leaves and zest, and basil or holy basil. Spices such as nutmeg, cloves and cinnamon are used occasionally, mostly in meat dishes. Spice pastes, known as *bumbu* in Indonesia and *rempah* in Malaysia, vary a lot: wet or dry, simple or elaborate with as many as twenty ingredients, lightly fried in oil or simmered in coconut milk. Cooked fish, shrimp paste or a condiment made from fermented salted fish are common additions.

In Indonesia curries are cooked with tomatoes and European vegetables planted in the highlands by the Dutch; onions, aubergines and cucumber introduced by Indians; and mustard greens, soy beans and tofu brought by the Chinese. *Sambal goreng*, which means 'fried relish', is an umbrella term for a category of curry-like dishes made from meat, seafood or vegetables flavoured with curry paste, with or without coconut milk.

In Western Sumatra Indian and Arab traders in ancient times introduced coriander, cumin, turmeric and cinnamon. Later, when South Indian indentured labourers from Malaysia went to Indonesia, they added Sumatran flavourings like lime leaves and galangal to their curries, creating a hybrid cuisine. In Pedang in Java, and the western and northern Malay Peninsula, beef rendang is the most famous; this can be mild and creamy, or spicier with a thick, semi-dry texture – there are multiple variations. Once voted the world's favourite curry, found all across Malaysia and also Singapore, it's gently simmered with cinnamon, cardamom, cloves, star anise, lemongrass, lime leaves, galangal, sun-dried tamarind slices, fresh coconut, coconut milk, candlenuts, turmeric leaves and dried red chillies.

The cuisine of Java is more delicate, balancing sweet, sour and hot flavours, and has a wide range of curries. *Gulai* are yellow curries cooked in coconut milk, and *ayams* are very spicy and eaten at Eid, to give two examples. Curries may additionally include green jackfruit, oilcakes, papaya leaves, cassava leaves, snails or fermented durian.

Women of mixed Javanese and Chinese heritage were known as Nonya and were renowned for their cooking. Later when Dutch women went to Indonesia to join their husbands, they created Dutch-Indonesian dishes like *kari jawa*, a beef and potato curry in coconut milk. Among the best-known in this category is *rijsttafel*, meaning 'rice table'. An elaborate *thali*-like meal of plain or coloured rice with several meat, fish and vegetable accompaniments, it was invented by Dutch planters in the late nineteenth century, probably based on a traditional Javanese ceremonial meal. *Rijsttafel* was served in a grand style for Sunday lunches, dinner parties and on steamships. It survives mainly as a tourist attraction in the Netherlands and its former colonies.

In Malaysia the Chinese came as traders in the sixteenth century, or were brought in by the British in the nineteenth century for jobs in tin mines. South Indians and Ceylonese were shipped in to work on rubber and palm-oil plantations, followed by civil servants. So the cuisine reflects this cultural mix.

During the sixteenth and seventeenth centuries Indian spice merchants took Gujarati and South Indian recipes to Malaysia, where they combined Indian spice mixes with star anise from Chinese traders and Malaysian lemongrass

to create coconut-based curries. Tamil rubber plantation workers introduced lentil dishes.

As northern Malaysia shares a border with Thailand, the food there has much in common with Thai food, while in the southeast, Javanese influences can be found. As in Indonesia, Malaysian women who married Chinese men were known as Nonya – or Peranakan – and were also famous for their cooking. They combined Chinese recipes with local ingredients like galangal, candlenuts, pandan leaves, lemongrass and lime leaves.

One of the most famous Nonya dishes is curry chicken kapitan. No relation to Anglo-Indian country captain chicken, it's named after a local figure of importance known as *kapitan*, who acted as a go-between for Chinese communities and Malaysian rulers. It's made by frying chicken pieces in a curry paste flavoured with anise and other spices, shallots, chillies and shrimp paste, and braising in coconut milk with fresh grated coconut, tamarind and cinnamon. Another renowned chicken curry is Indian-influenced *kari ayam*, cooked with curry powder, curry leaves and star anise.

Singaporean curries may also contain curry powder and curry leaves, along with pandan leaves, coconut milk, potatoes, shallots and whole spices such as cinnamon sticks.

THAILAND

The Thai word for curry is *kaeng*, which means a dish with gravy thickened by curry paste, or the curry paste itself. The essential ingredients are onions or shallots, garlic, chillies and shrimp paste. Coconut milk isn't always used and is rare in northern Thai cooking. Indian-style curries with spices are known as *kari*.

Thai curries are cooked with meat, chicken, seafood, vegetables including various local leafy greens, bamboo shoots, fruits such as bananas and sometimes frogs, snails, snakes, wild birds and game meats like sambar deer or wild boar.

Traditionally the ingredients for a curry paste were pounded together for a long time in a stone mortar to release their flavour and aroma. Most contain shrimp paste made from salted sun-dried shrimps that have been powdered and fermented, or boiled or roasted on banana leaves before use.

Other ingredients may include grachai (wild ginger that's stronger in taste than galangal), coriander root, makrut lime leaves, holy basil, tamarind, palm sugar and spices such as cardamon and cumin. Aubergines of varying sizes can also be found. The aim is to balance hot, sour, sweet and salty elements; no one flavour should dominate.

Outside Thailand, red curries flavoured with dried red chillies, and green curries made from fresh green chillies and holy basil, are the best known. However, there are several other varieties, including yellow curry coloured with turmeric and curry powder; Penang containing dried red chillies, white peppercorns and sometimes peanuts; and massaman with peanuts and roasted whole spices such as star anise, cinnamon and cardamom. Massaman is a Muslim curry that originated near the Malaysian border where there is a sizeable Muslim population, but interestingly a 'mussaman' curry is also mentioned in *Ain I Akbari*. They're completely different, with their Muslim background the only common element.

JAPAN

The Japanese are extremely passionate about curry, which is surprising given that Japan was never a colony, nor did it have indentured labourers.

Until the 1860s Japan had been socially, culturally and commercially isolated from the rest of the world for a couple of hundred years. The new rulers of the Meiji (1868–1912) and, later, Taisho (1912–26) eras set about modernising the country, actively promoting Western culture and technology. The British were now allowed to import various new and unfamiliar foods, which included Anglo-Indian curries and curry powder.

The earliest Japanese curries mirrored Anglo-Indian versions, made from curry powder roux, stock, cream and lemon juice. They were categorised as *yoshoku* – Western foods made according to local tastes – and coveted by the rising middle classes, who saw them as symbols of progress. Over time, the roux was replaced by curry blocks, now a distinctive feature of Japanese curry-making. These blocks are made from flour, fat, curry powder, Japanese condiments and dashi stock.

Curries were such a hit that they were served in Japan-bound steamships, restaurants and department stores. The army promoted them as a modern Western dish to attract new recruits. They could be made in large batches and were considered ideal for increasing meat consumption, newly encouraged due to its association with strength. The army and navy were instrumental in popularising them. The navy curry, called *kaigun kare*, is made with beef or chicken, onions, potatoes, carrots, curry roux and pickled vegetables.

Kare raisu (curry and rice) is one of the best-loved dishes in Japan and is sold everywhere. Chicken, meat or fish is cooked with onions, potatoes and carrots in a curry sauce sweetened with apples or honey. There are many other varieties, and some regional ones are made from sika deer, scallops, natto, whale, pears or bitter melon. There are even some made from cheese, bananas or frankfurters; they come in various heat levels.

Indian-style curries are known as Nakamuraya, as they were introduced by the Hindu nationalist Rash Behari Bose (1886–1945) and sold at his father-in-law's bakery named after Bose's wife, Nakamuraya. Although there are Indo-ryori restaurants that serve Indian curries, many Japanese prefer their Anglo-Indian versions.

MAURITIUS

Two-thirds of the population here is made up of the descendants of indentured workers: a few Muslims but mostly Hindus, the majority from Northeast India. The island has been colonised in turn by the Dutch, French and British, and is home to people from French Creole and Chinese backgrounds. The cuisine reflects all these influences. There's a version of vindaloo called *vindaille*, made from seafood marinated with saffron, mustard, chillies, garlic and vinegar. *Cari masala poule* is a well-known chicken curry cooked with potatoes, tomatoes, curry powder, green chillies, cinnamon, curry leaves and thyme.

SOUTH AFRICA

South African cuisine is a combination of African, Dutch (later Afrikaaner), British, French, Malaysian and Indian. In the mid-seventeenth century, the Dutch East India Company established a settlement, like a modern-day truck stop, at the Cape of Good Hope to provide food and other essentials to ships sailing between the Netherlands and the East Indies. The officials were from Dutch, French,

Huguenot and German backgrounds, and brought over slaves from India and Indonesia to work in the settlements' farms and kitchens. These slaves and their children became known as Cape Malays, most of whom now live in Cape Town. The Cape Malays' cooking skills were in high demand, and spices from Indonesia were heavily used in curries known as *kerries*.

Then, over 150 years later, the British got control of the Cape and brought in thousands of indentured labourers to work on their sugar, banana, tea and coffee plantations. Most were from South India, but some came from Bihar, Orissa and Uttar Pradesh. By the end of the century, Indian businessmen, retailers and lawyers arrived, mainly from Gujarat, and set up cafés and grocery stores.

By this time Cape Malay dishes had largely lost their Dutch influence and had become more Asian. *Kerries* are flavoured with mild curry powder and freshly ground spices, and can be sweet and sour with the addition of mango or peach chutney, apricots or other fruit, and lemon juice or vinegar. There are also *giema* (keema), *groema* (korma) and Pinang (Penang) curries.

During apartheid Cape Malay food wasn't allowed in mainstream restaurants, so had to be sold in 'cook-shops'. Indians, known as *bunny* – thought to be derived from *bania*, the merchant caste who worked in Durban as traders – set up small cafés selling rice and curry. It was illegal to serve Indian food to Black South Africans, so the restaurateurs hid curries in hollowed-out bread rolls and handed them over surreptitiously at the back door to be eaten without cutlery. This is how the famous dish bunny chow – meaning 'Indian food' – was born.

The largest Indian population is said to be in Durban, where one of the most famous dishes is Durban curry. It's a fiery hot chicken or meat dish with potatoes, tomatoes, cinnamon, curry masala (different from curry powder) and curry leaves.

TRINIDAD AND TOBAGO, GUYANA, JAMAICA

Most Indian labourers in Trinidad were from Uttar Pradesh and Bihar. They cooked with their daily rations of rice, dal, coconut oil or ghee, turmeric and sometimes onions and salted or dried fish. They toasted spices like cumin, coriander and fenugreek, so their curries had a dark hue. They used culantro (also known as saw-tooth coriander) as a substitute for coriander and callaloo for spinach and mustard leaves.

Trini curry chicken with potatoes is a much-loved dish flavoured with chillies, curry powder, garam masala, cumin and a green curry paste made from fresh coriander, culantro, parsley, thyme, spring onions, green bell peppers, assorted green chillies and lemon juice.

Some curries are eaten stuffed inside *rotis* as fast food. The most common include fish, meat or vegetable curries stuffed into yellow pea *rotis*, and doubles, in which curried chickpeas are enveloped inside two turmeric-yellow flatbreads. Often served with pickles and relishes, so important are curries in the Trinidadian diet that they've been immortalised in songs.

Guyanese curries are similar, sometimes with the addition of local wiri wiri chillies, and green mangoes used as a souring agent.

In Jamaica, chives, parsley and thyme once introduced by Europeans are widely used, along with Scotch bonnet – the original chilli 'discovered' by Columbus in 1492. Indian-influenced dishes like curry goat, *roti* and callaloo are also staples. Curry goat is cooked with coconut milk and curry powder and eaten with rice and peas. Jamaican curry chicken, served with hot sauce, is a combination of potatoes, curry powder, allspice, coconut milk, white wine vinegar, thyme and Scotch bonnet.

AMERICA

Before the American Revolution (1765–84) wealthy Americans ordered Indian spices via England or the Caribbean, including pepper, ginger, cardamom, saffron, turmeric, cumin and curry powder. Then in 1809 India Wharf opened in Boston for ships to bring imports from Calcutta. By the 1830s, chicken curry, lobster curry and curried veal had become commonplace in Boston's waterside taverns and restaurants.

The first curry recipes appeared in a regional American cookbook, *The Virginia Housewife, or Methodical Cook* (1824) by Mary Randolph (1762–1828), which lists chicken curry 'after the East India manner', catfish curry and curry powder. Like Anglo-Indian curries, early American curries contained apples, bananas and sultanas. I have even seen modern recipes that include fresh or evaporated milk, salted peanuts, bacon bits, cranberries and Coca-Cola.

In the 1890s a small number of young, uneducated agricultural workers arrived in California from Punjab to work on fruit and vegetable farms, railways and in lumber mills. The idea was to earn money to support their families back home and return as quickly as possible. The immigration laws changed in 1917, making it harder for them to stay. The few who remained married local Mexican women and started a community of 'Mexican Hindus'; from this a 'Mexican-Hindu' cuisine was born. It took common elements from both cultures and fused them into one. This food was served in Californian restaurants from the 1910s to the 1930s, very few of which survive today.

One of the first American celebrity chefs was an Indian cook in the early twentieth century named Ranji Smile. He entranced New York society with his curry-making skills, dashing good looks, extravagant costumes, exotic tales and increasingly wild claims about being a prince, friend of royalty and a Cambridge graduate. Smile's story is fascinating and complicated but, having made his mark, his downfall was swift. Success went to his head and he was arrested for drunken and disorderly behaviour as well as for bringing in and exploiting illegal labourers. He became a womaniser and eventually disappeared in 1913, either to open a restaurant in Delhi or to lead a quiet life somewhere in America. More than just a conman, though, he was an intelligent victim of a hostile society, trying to find his way and make his mark in an industry suspicious of foreigners. He was given to self-mythologising, as many publicity-savvy chefs are today – though perhaps not to such a dramatic degree.

Due to stringent immigration laws America's Indian population was small, mostly students in New York, but by the mid-twentieth century Indian restaurants had grown in number. Because Americans had little contact with Indians they romanticised the cuisine, with various food writers calling curry 'rare Oriental ragout', 'incredibly involved for the average Occidental', 'made ... from between twenty to forty spices' and 'the true foods of Occult India'.

After the Second World War Sylheti sailors who had jumped ship and settled in New York married Puerto Rican or African American women and opened Indian cafés. There isn't the same history of Bangladeshi-owned restaurants as in Britain though; after immigration laws relaxed further in 1965, it was mostly Indian middle-class professionals who opened restaurants.

In 1964, New York's World's Fair raised an awareness of Indian food; this impressed the legendary restaurant critic

Craig Claiborne (1920–2000), who went on to review several Indian restaurants. Today Indian food isn't as sought after as Mexican or Chinese, and the word curry isn't used as widely as in Britain. Instead, what has become hugely popular is a variety of Indian street-food snacks called *chaat*.

LAST WORDS

As we now know curry and curry powder have travelled the world and become incorporated into various international cuisines, reflecting the movement of ingredients and the creation of new dishes since the dawn of time.

Those who want to cancel the word curry are already too late. Try telling a Japanese schoolboy tucking into his *kari raisu* or a Trinidadian street vendor selling curry-stuffed *roti* that the dish they love doesn't exist. An Indian telling an Anglo-Indian that 'our curries are more authentic than yours' would be the height of arrogance, so let's not get too precious about curry.

A bigger issue is that anyone rejecting the term curry because of its association with colonialism must – by logic – also reject ingredients brought to India by colonials, such as potatoes, tomatoes, chillies and bread. So is anyone prepared to make the cuisine less delicious in order to make a political point? Incidentally some older Hindus and right-wing nationalists also want to strip Indian food of all foreign names and influences … to do what? Restore it to the time when Indians ate barley gruel and rice porridge? So here we have widely different ideologies ostensibly aiming for the same thing.

It's too late because India has already fully embraced the term curry. Curry recipes have been published in cookbooks and magazines for decades. Curries are cooked in restaurants and homes and are – yes – called curry. Even the classic Anglo-Indian-Bangladeshi curries are found on menus in India, billed as British-style curries.

It's too late also because the perception of Indian food has already been changing. Many non-Indians have enthusiastically embraced *chaat*, *dosas*, *samosas* and all kinds of other non-curry items. Perhaps it was necessary to emphasise that there's more to Indian food in the 1970s, but this is no longer the case. The discourses about authenticity, culinary appropriation and decolonising food are not so straightforward.

We're nearing the end of our book on curry … but there's something missing. The story of curry is rather one-sided. From the earliest Greek, Chinese, Portuguese and British travellers, to the French and American anthropologists of the twentieth century, to the British and American academics and food historians of recent years, it's a tale as told mostly by non-Indians, and occasionally the Indian diaspora – which includes me. Where are the voices of Indians living in India? During the time that curry developed in Britain, how did it evolve in the subcontinent?

One reason for this gap is that food writing, food history and food anthropology are relatively new disciplines in the subcontinent. Other obstacles are to do with limited funding for research, lack of resources and persistent misinformation and mythologising of many aspects of the cuisine. Many historic texts and family and community cookbooks are locked away in the safes of the surviving royal families, or they might be written in one of the many Indian languages unfamiliar to the Indian food historian.

Indians haven't just been passive recipients of colonial influences, either. We have absorbed and used many aspects, which in turn have significantly affected the way the cuisine has changed. I would love to hear the stories of the cooks who worked in the colonial kitchens, grumbling and burping, giving their masters hard stares, deliberately masala-fying their English recipes, or stealing headstones from their cemeteries to grind spices (yes, that did happen). I would love to read books by the Bengalis who wrote disapprovingly about their British sahibs' eating habits.

I would love to talk to the early Bangladeshi restaurateurs who felt compelled to dumb down recipes so much that they couldn't even eat in their own restaurants. I would love to hear about the soft-spoken waiters who – when faced with hostility or violence – put on a servile manner just to earn some tips.

Most of all, I would love to know about curries beyond what the Mughal elites were eating because – like in many countries around the world – the cuisine that is recorded the most systematically is that of the aristocracy. Which curries are the everyday fare of Dalits, Adivasis and various other marginalised groups and tribes? What are the specialities of regions like, say, Northeast India that few people outside those boundaries know about? What are their stories? I hope we get to read them some day.

NOTES

1 YouGov, 'The Most Popular Dishes (Q3 2021)', https://yougov.
co.uk/ratings/food/popularity/dishes/all; YouGov, 'The
UK's Favourite Takeaways 2021', https://yougov.co.uk/topics
/food/articles-reports/2021/02/05/what-britains-favourite
-takeaway; YouGov, 'Italian cuisine is the world's most
popular 2019' https://yougov.co.uk/topics/food/articles
-reports/2019/03/12/italian-cuisine-worlds-most-popular;
YouGov, 'Poppadominant: Korma revealed to be Britain's
favourite curry 2016', https://yougov.co.uk/topics/lifestyle
/articles-reports/2016/11/29/poppadominant-korma-revealed
-be-britains-favourite. All accessed on 10 October 2021.
2 CNN, 'The World's 50 Best Foods', https://edition.cnn.com
/travel/article/world-best-food-dishes/index.html. Accessed
on 10 October 2021.
3 See, for example, 'Calls to boycott the word "curry" over claims
it is rooted in British colonialism', *Evening Standard*,
9 August 2021, https://www.standard.co.uk/news/uk/calls
-cancel-curry-british-colonialism-chaheti-bansal-b949843
.html. Accessed on 10 October 2021.
4 Madhur Jaffrey, *An Invitation To Indian Cooking* (London,
Arrow Books, 2003), pp. 14–15.
5 Mudaliar C. Rasanayagam, *Ancient Jaffna* (Madras: Everyman's
Publishers Ltd, 1926), pp. 140–60.

6 K. T. Achaya, *Indian Food: A Historical Companion* (New Delhi, Oxford University Press, 1994), p. 90.

7 Flora Annie Steel, *The Complete Indian Housekeeper and Cook*, (London: William Heinemann, 1913, first edition 1888), p. 305.

8 Extract from Arthur Robert Kenney-Herbert, *Culinary Jottings for Madras* (1878), as reported in *The Calcutta Review*, 1879, Volume 68, p. xiii.

9 Eliza Acton, *Modern Cookery For Private Families* (London: Longman, Brown, Green & Longmans, 1845), pp. 296–7.

10 Lizzie Collingham, *Curry: A Tale of Cooks and Conquerors*, London: Vintage Books, 2006), p. 227.

11 BBC News, 'Peers say citizenship test should focus on essential knowledge, not trivia', 18 April 2018, https://www.bbc.co.uk /news/uk-politics-43807963; iNews, 'Two-thirds of Brits would fail the UK citizenship test which asks questions like: How tall is the London Eye?', 15 January 2021, https://inews .co.uk/news/uk/two-thirds-brits-would-fail-uk-citizenship -test-questions-height-london-eye-831594. Both accessed on 17 September 2021.

12 YouGov, 'What do Britons like most on their chips?' 2020 survey https://yougov.co.uk/topics/food/articles-reports /2020/08/14/what-do-britons-most-their-chips. Accessed on 10 October 2021.

13 Lizzie Collingham, *Curry: A Tale of Cooks and Conquerors*, p. 221.

14 Anonymous ('A Thirty-Five Years' Resident'), *The Indian Cookery Book: The Practical Handbook to the Kitchen in India*; Calcutta, Wyman & Co, 1880, p. 22.

15 C. Herman Senn, *Ideal Breakfast Dishes, Savouries and Curries* (London: The Food and Cookery Publishing Agency, reprinted in 2018), p. 55.

FURTHER READING

K. T. Achaya, *Indian Food: A Historical Companion* (New Delhi: Oxford University Press, 1994)

K. T. Achaya, *A Historical Dictionary of Indian Food* (New Delhi: Oxford University Press, 1998)

K. T. Achaya, *The Illustrated Foods of India A–Z* (New Delhi: Oxford University Press, 2009)

Henry Yule and A. C. Burnell, *Hobson-Jobson: The Definitive Glossary of British India* (Oxford: Oxford University Press, 2015)

Lizzie Collingham, *Curry: A Tale of Cooks and Conquerors* (London: Vintage Books, 2006)

Colleen Taylor Sen, *Curry: A Global History* (London: Reaktion Books, 2009)

David Burnett and Helen Saberi, *The Road to Vindaloo: Curry Cooks and Curry Books* (Devon: Prospect Books, 2008)

Edited by Krishnendu Ray and Tulasi Srinivas, *Curried Cultures: Indian Food in the Age of Globalisation* (New Delhi: Aleph Book Company, 2017)

Naben Ruthnum, *Curry: Eating, Reading and Race* (Melbourne: The Text Publishing Company, 2017)

David Burton, *The Raj at Table: A Cultural History of the British in India* (India: Rupa & Co, 1995)

David Smith, *The Cooking Colonel of Madras* (Lulu.com, 2018)

E. P. Veerasawmy, *Indian Cookery For Use In All Countries* (Mumbai: Jaico Publishing House, 1956)

Chitrita Banerji, *Eating India: Exploring a Nation's Cuisine* (India: Penguin Books, 2008)

Madhur Jaffrey, *An Invitation to Indian Cooking* (London: Arrow Books, 2003)

LIST OF ILLUSTRATIONS

106

Also available in this series

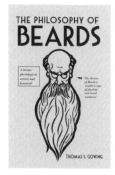

THE PHILOSOPHY OF
BEARDS

THOMAS S. GOWING

THE PHILOSOPHY OF
COFFEE

BRIAN WILLIAMS

THE PHILOSOPHY OF
WINE

RUTH BALL

THE PHILOSOPHY OF
TEA

TONY GEBELY

THE PHILOSOPHY OF
GIN

JANE PEYTON

THE PHILOSOPHY OF
CHEESE

PATRICK McGUIGAN

THE PHILOSOPHY OF
BEER

JANE PEYTON

THE PHILOSOPHY OF
TATTOOS

JOHN MILLER

THE PHILOSOPHY OF
WHISKY

BILLY ABBOTT